PIANO SOLO

MANNHEIM STEAMROLLER
Christmas SONG

ISBN 13: 978-1-4234-5290-4
ISBN 10: 1-4234-5290-9

DOTS AND LINES, INK

9130 MORMON BRIDGE ROAD OMAHA, NEBRASKA 68152 402.457.4341

DISTRIBUTED BY

HAL•LEONARD®
CORPORATION
7777 W. BLUEMOUND RD. P.O. BOX 13819 MILWAUKEE, WI 53213

LET IT SNOW! LET IT SNOW! LET IT SNOW!

Words by SAMMY CAHN
Music by JULE STYNE
Arranged by CHIP DAVIS

To Coda ⊕

Play 5 times

cresc. poco a poco

f

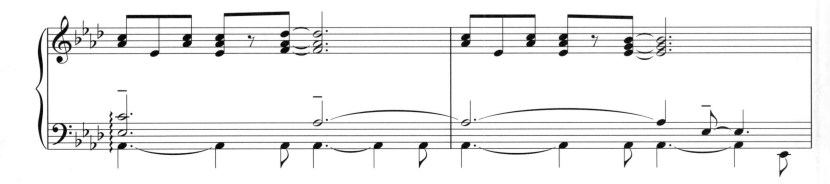

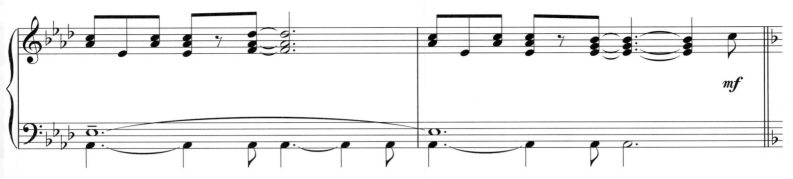

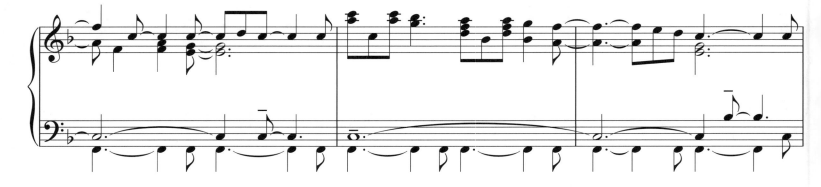

D.S. al Coda

CODA

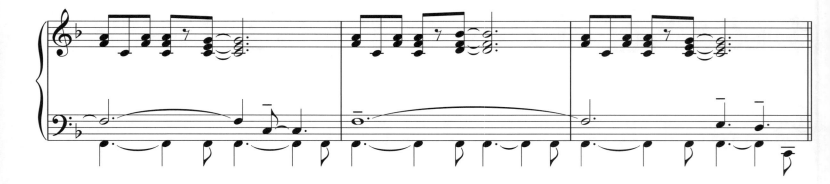

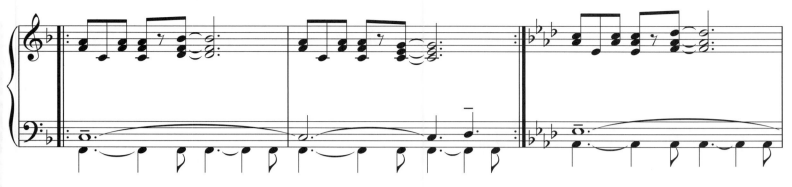

Repeat and Fade | **Optional Ending**

THE CHRISTMAS SONG
(Chestnuts Roasting on an Open Fire)

Music and Lyric by MEL TORME
and ROBERT WELLS
Arranged by CHIP DAVIS

Slowly, with warmth

folks dressed up ___ like Es - ki - mos. Ev-'ry-bod-y

knows a tur - key ___ and some mis - tle - toe

help to make the sea - son bright.

Ti - ny tots ___ with their eyes all a - glow ___ will ___

find it hard to sleep to-night. They know that San - ta's on his way; he's load-ed lots of toys and good-ies on his sleigh. And ev-'ry moth-er's child is gon-na spy to see if

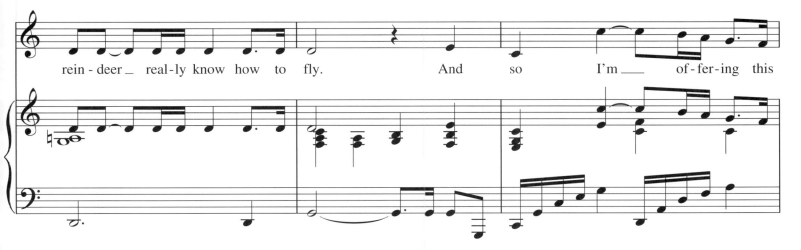

rein - deer _ real-ly know how to fly. And so I'm _ of-fer-ing this

sim-ple phrase _ to kids from one to nine-ty-two; al-

though it's been said man-y times, man-y ways, _ mer-ry Christ-mas, mer-ry

Christ-mas, mer - ry Christ-mas _ to _ you.

SANTA CLAUS IS COMIN' TO TOWN

Words by HAVEN GILLESPIE
Music by J. FRED COOTS
Arranged by CHIP DAVIS

Bright Jazzy Swing

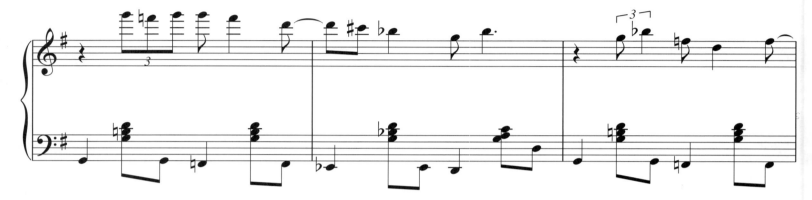

sim.

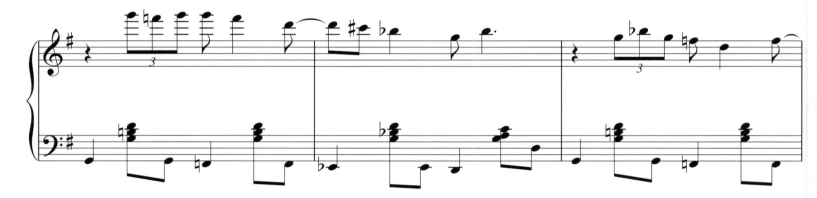

Repeat and Fade

Optional Ending

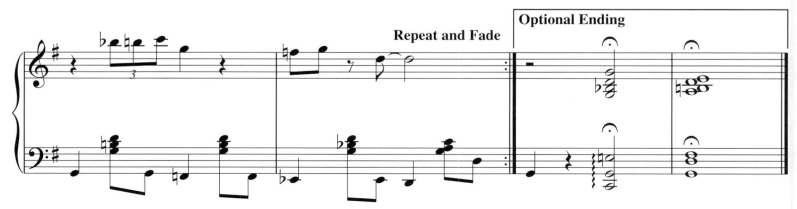

IT CAME UPON A MIDNIGHT CLEAR

Words by EDMUND HAMILTON SEARS
Music by RICHARD STORRS WILLIS
Arranged by CHIP DAVIS

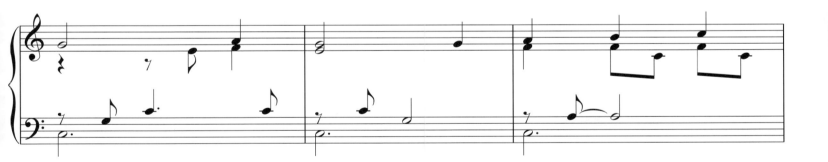

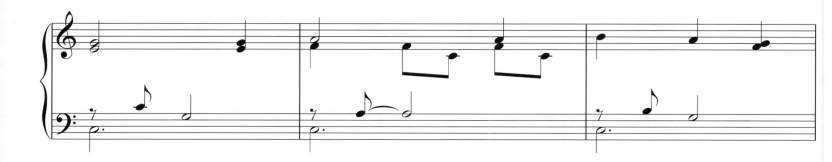

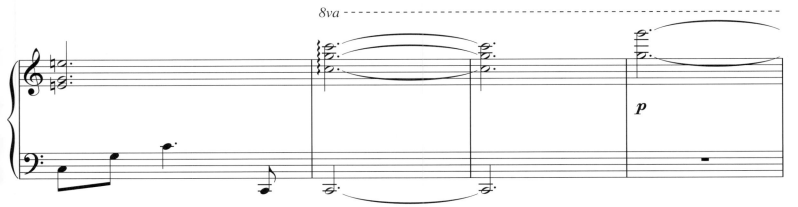

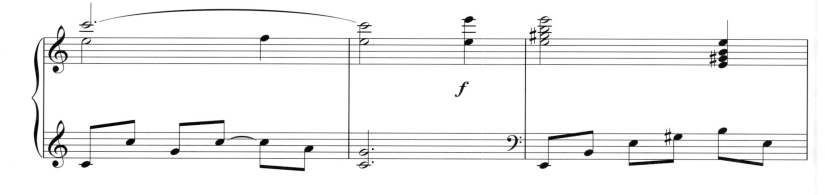

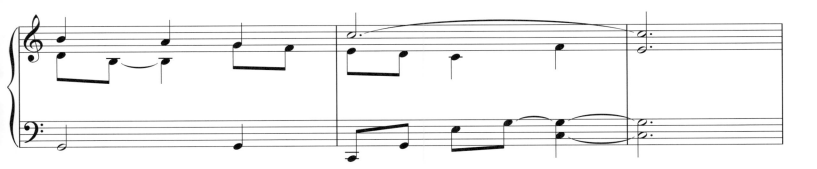

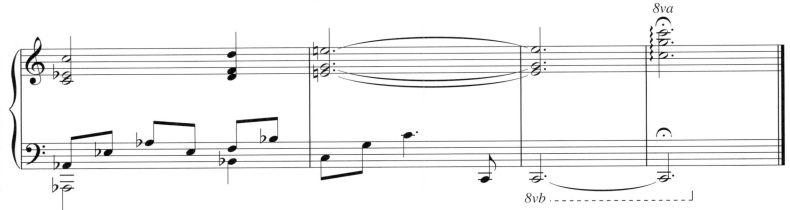

FELIZ NAVIDAD

Music and Lyrics by JOSÉ FELICIANO
Arranged by CHIP DAVIS

Joyfully

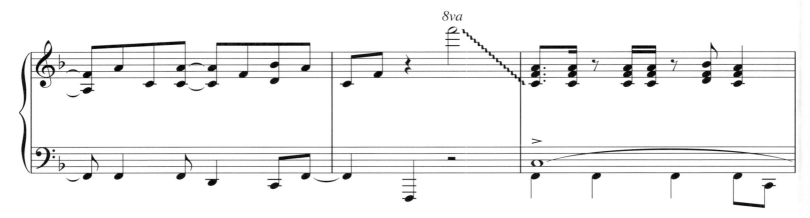

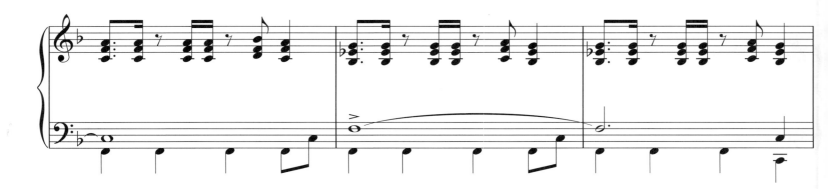

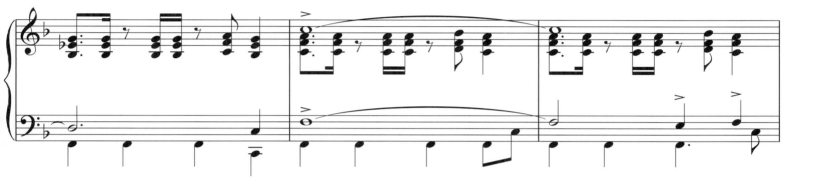

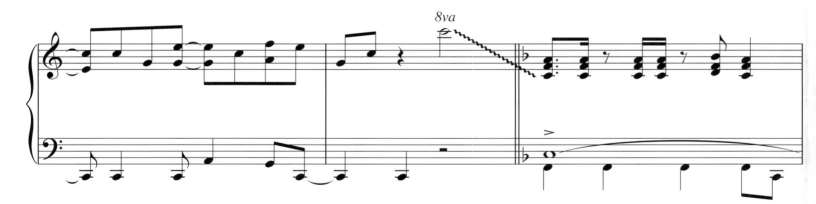

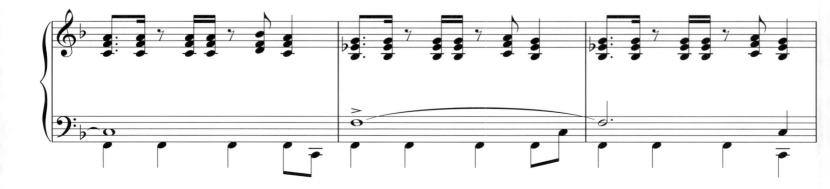

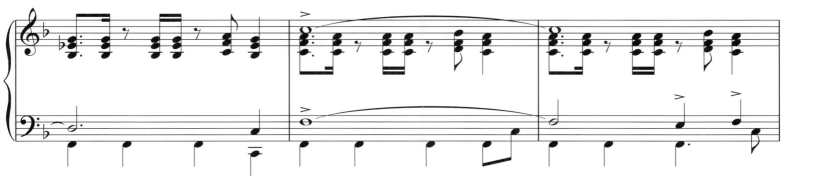

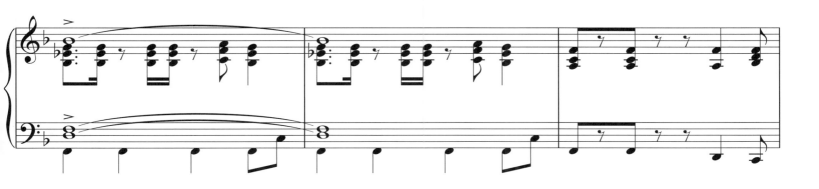

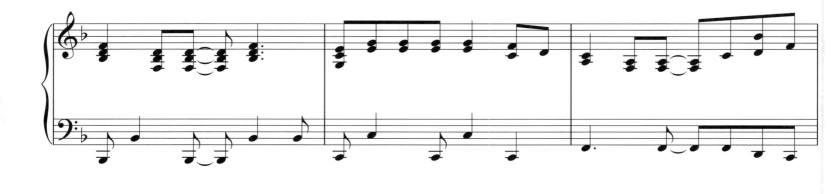

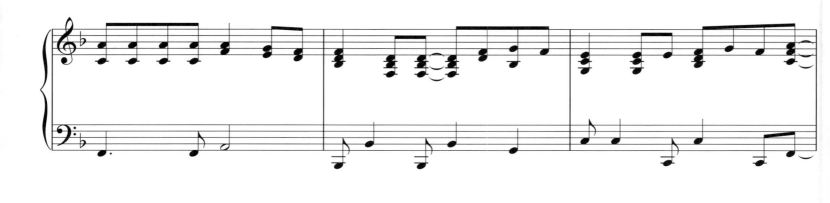

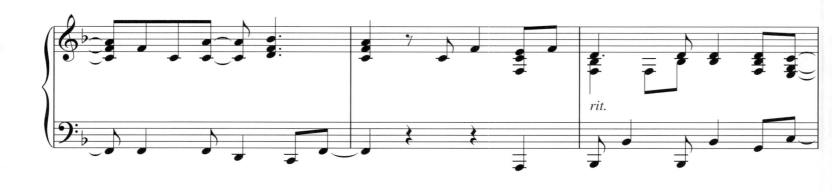

CATCHING SNOWFLAKES ON YOUR TONGUE

By CHIP DAVIS

Moderately fast, flowing

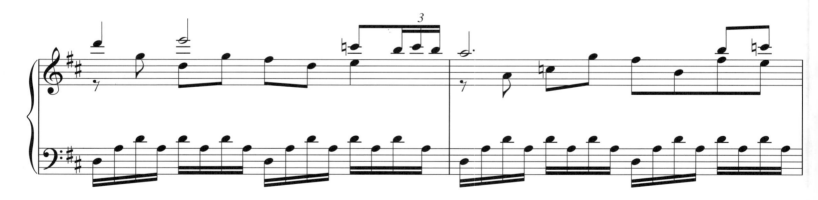

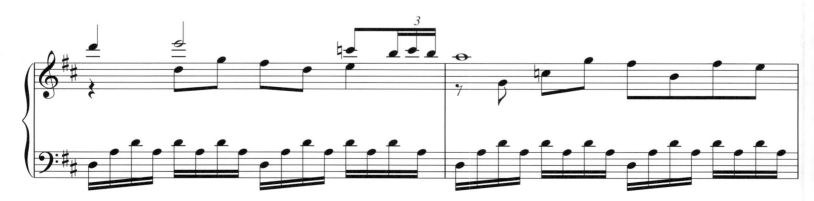

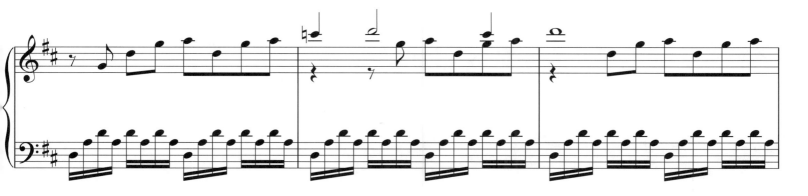

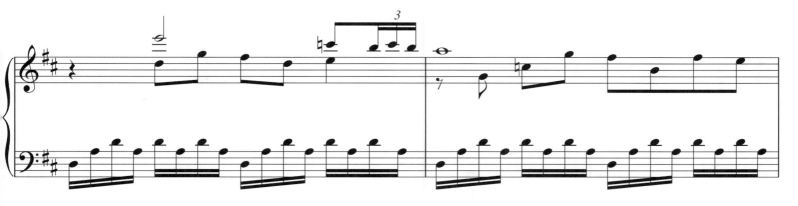

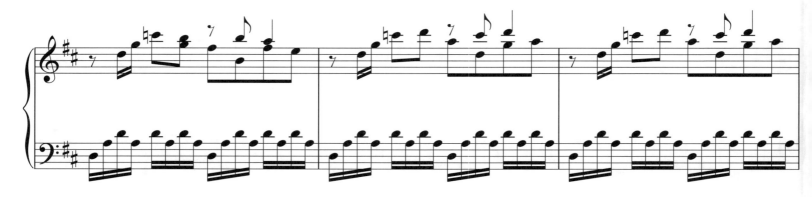

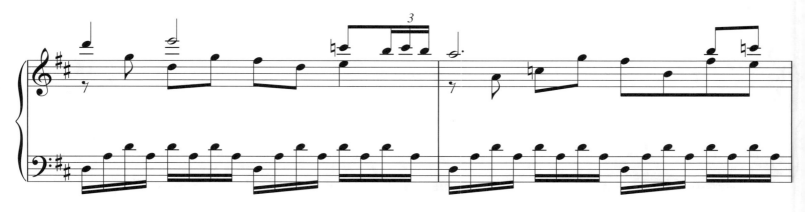

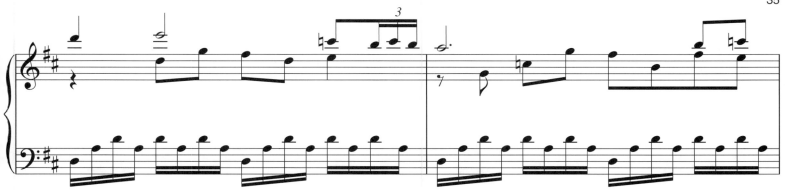

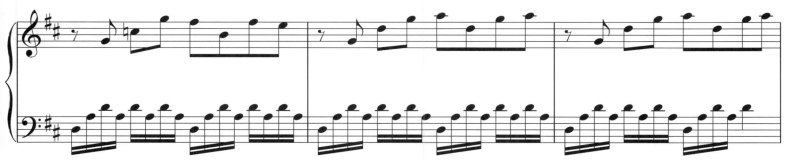

Repeat and Fade | **Optional Ending**

MASTERS IN THE HALL

By WILLIAM MORRIS
and RICHARD STORRS WILLIS
Arranged by CHIP DAVIS

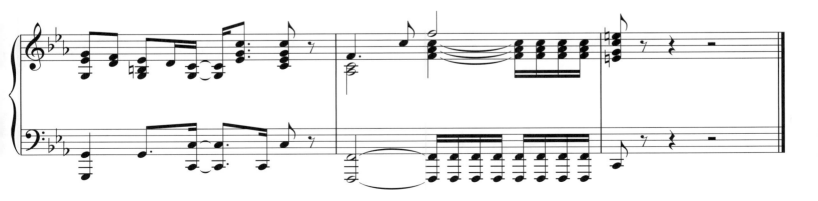

ABOVE THE NORTHERN LIGHTS

Music by CHIP DAVIS
Lyrics by ED WILSON

Moderately slow, dreamily

Up a-bove the North-ern Lights on Christ - mas night,
Leg-ends say that spir - its dance a - cross the sky.

shim-mer - ing a - bove the clouds, dreams take flight.
Chil-dren sing and sleigh bells ring, rein - deer fly.

1.

Mag - ic fills _____ the _ air,

spir - its ev - - 'ry - where.

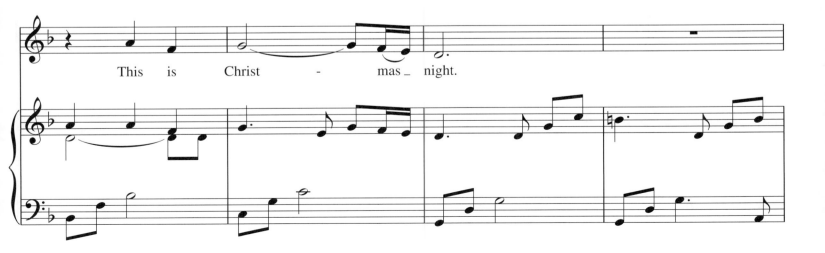

This is Christ - mas _ night.

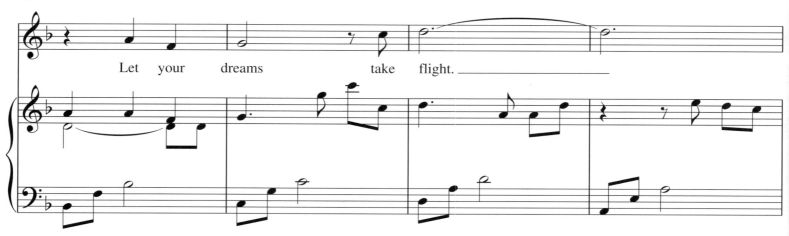

Let your dreams take flight. _____

Up a - bove the North-ern Lights on
You and I be - neath the sky be -

Christ - mas night, trav - el - ing through
hold the light. Qui - et - ly, the

space and time,   end - less   light.
mys - ter - y   fills   the

1.

2.

night.

Mag - ic   fills _____ the _ air,

spir - its ev - 'ry - where.

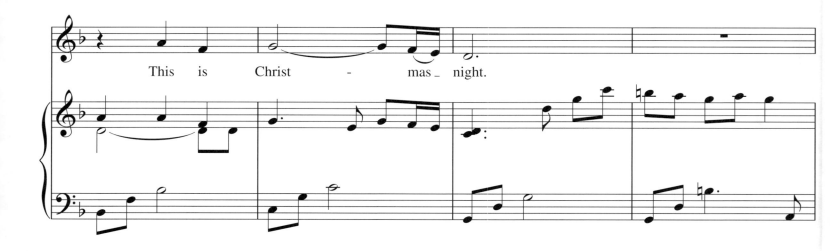

This is Christ - mas night.

Let your dreams take flight.

mp

Up a-bove the North-ern Lights on Christ - mas night, shim - mer - ing a - bove the clouds, dreams take flight.

pp

rit.

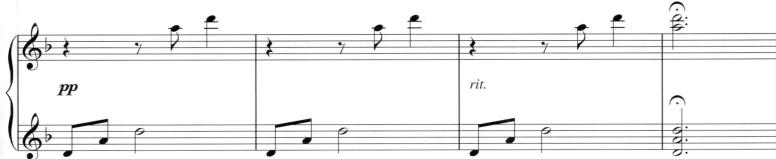

FROSTY THE SNOW MAN

Words and Music by STEVE NELSON
and JACK ROLLINS
Arranged by CHIP DAVIS

Moderate Techno

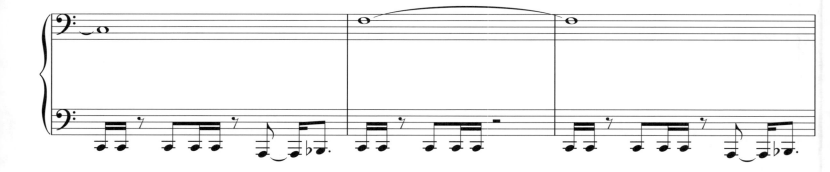

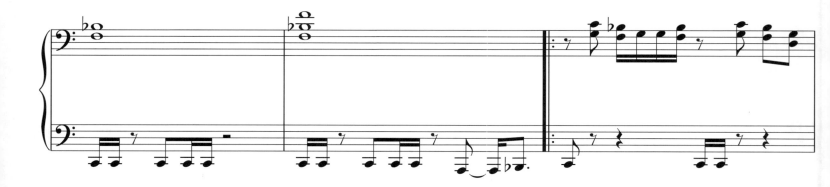

D.S. al Coda

CODA

Play 7 times

TRADITIONS OF CHRISTMAS
(Music Box)

Words and Music by CHIP DAVIS

Moderately, simply

CHRISTMAS LULLABY

Music by CHIP DAVIS
Lyrics by ED WILSON

Simply

Sleep tight, little one, Christ-mas day is all

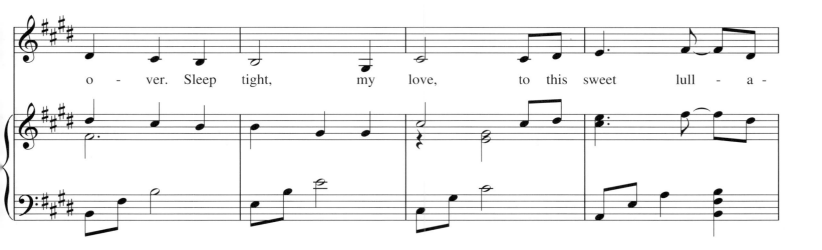

o - ver. Sleep tight, my love, to this sweet lull - a -

by. All the stars in the sky will keep watch o - ver

your heart. All the stars _____ and I will keep watch o - ver

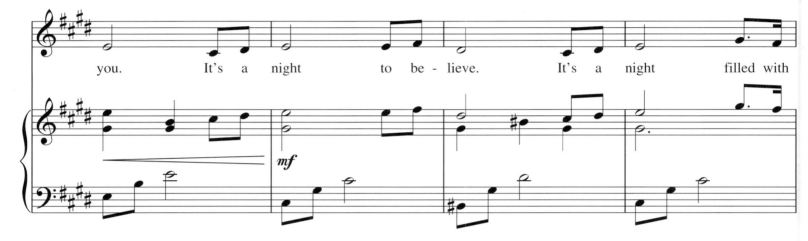

you. It's a night to be - lieve. It's a night filled with

mf

won - der. It's a night filled with dreams, Christ-mas dreams, you can

cresc.

make true. _____ All the stars in the sky will keep

decresc.   *mp*

watch o - ver your heart. All the an - gels and I will keep

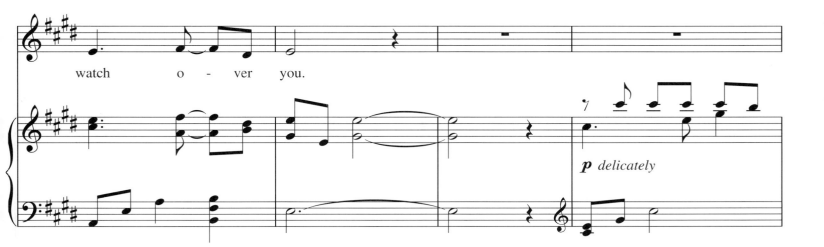

watch o - ver you.

p delicately

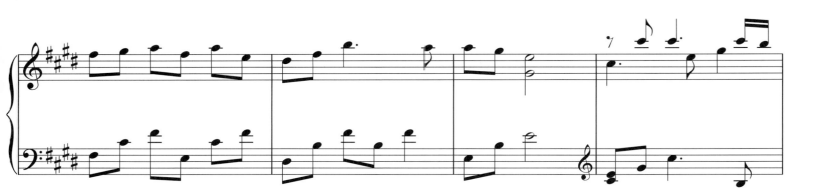

Sleep

tight, lit - tle one, Christ - mas day is all o - ver. Your

sonorous

dad - dy and I will __ al - ways __ love you. It's a

p

night to be - lieve. It's a night filled with won - der. It's a

night filled with dreams, Christ-mas dreams, you can make true. ___

Sleep, lit - tle one, Christ-mas day is all o - ver. Your

dad - dy and I will ___ al - ways love you. _____

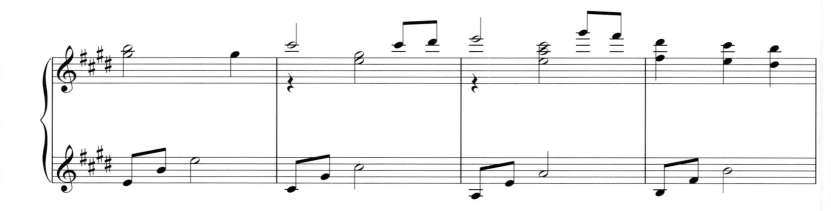

HAVE YOURSELF A MERRY LITTLE CHRISTMAS

Words and Music by HUGH MARTIN
and RALPH BLANE
Arranged by CHIP DAVIS

Slowly

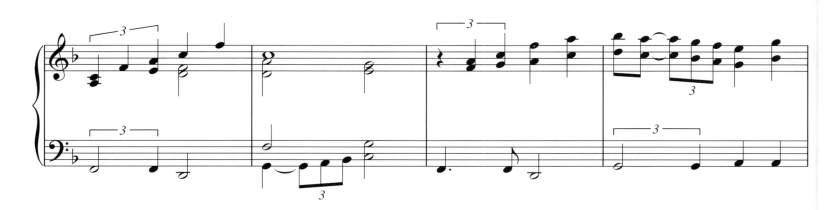

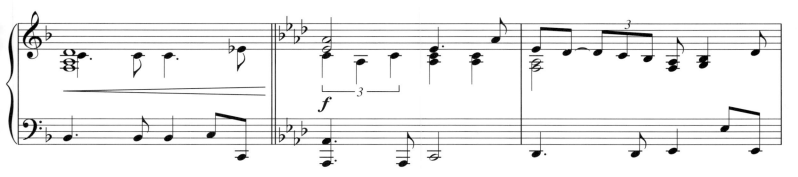

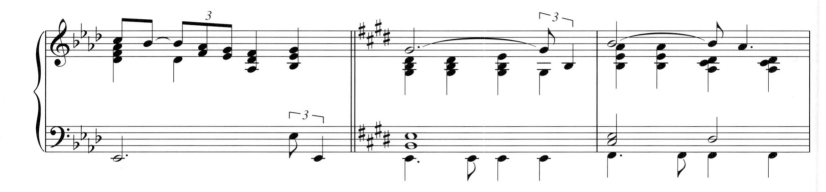